FALLING MAN and OTHER MONOLOGUES

BY WILL SCHEFFER

★

DRAMATISTS
PLAY SERVICE
INC.

FALLING MAN and OTHER MONOLOGUES
Copyright © 1999, Will Scheffer
All Rights Reserved

CAUTION: Professionals and amateurs are hereby warned that performance of FALLING MAN and Other Monologues is subject to a royalty. It is fully protected under the copyright laws of the United States of America, and of all countries covered by the International Copyright Union (including the Dominion of Canada and the rest of the British Commonwealth), and of all countries covered by the Pan-American Copyright Convention, the Universal Copyright Convention, the Berne Convention, and of all countries with which the United States has reciprocal copyright relations. All rights, including professional/amateur stage rights, motion picture, recitation, lecturing, public reading, radio broadcasting, television, video or sound recording, all other forms of mechanical or electronic reproduction, such as CD-ROM, CD-I, DVD, information storage and retrieval systems and photocopying, and the rights of translation into foreign languages, are strictly reserved. Particular emphasis is placed upon the matter of readings, permission for which must be secured from the Author's agent in writing.

The stage performance rights in FALLING MAN and Other Monologues (other than first class rights) are controlled exclusively by the DRAMATISTS PLAY SERVICE, INC., 440 Park Avenue South, New York, N.Y. 10016. No professional or non-professional performance of the Play (excluding first class professional performance) may be given without obtaining in advance the written permission of the DRAMATISTS PLAY SERVICE, INC., and paying the requisite fee.

Inquiries concerning all other rights should be addressed to Berman, Boals & Flynn, 208 West 30th Street, Suite 401, New York, N.Y. 10001, Attn: Judy Boals.

SPECIAL NOTE

Anyone receiving permission to produce FALLING MAN and Other Monologues is required (1) to give credit to the Author as sole and exclusive Author of the Play on the title page of all programs distributed in connection with performances of the Play and in all instances in which the title of the Play appears for purposes of advertising, publicizing or otherwise exploiting the Play and/or a production thereof. The name of the Author must appear on a separate line, in which no other name appears, immediately beneath the title and in size of type equal to 50% of the largest, most prominent letter used for the title of the Play. No person, firm or entity may receive credit larger or more prominent than that accorded the Author; and (2) if the entire collection of monologues is produced, or either one or both of FALLING MAN or TENNESSEE AND ME, to give the following acknowledgment on the title page of all programs distributed in connection with performances of the Play:

FALLING MAN was originally produced by The Ensemble Studio Theatre,
Curt Demptster, Artistic Director; Kevin Confoy, Executive Producer.

TENNESSEE AND ME was originally produced by The Ensemble Studio Theatre,
Curt Demptster, Artistic Director; Jamie Richards, Executive Producer.

SPECIAL NOTE ON SONGS AND RECORDINGS

For performance of the songs, arrangements and recordings mentioned in this Play that are protected by copyright, the permission of the copyright owners must be obtained; or other songs, arrangements and recordings in the public domain substituted.

TABLE OF CONTENTS

ALIEN BOY 5
FIRE DANCE 17
TENNESSEE AND ME 25
ONE MAN'S MEAT 35
FALLING MAN 45

ALIEN BOY

ALIEN BOY

Sousa march* blares as the lights fade. Lights up on a boy in a sailor suit.

ALIEN BOY.   Today I am thirteen. *(Sound: a nuclear bomb exploding.)*

I don't want to be thirteen. I have always yearned to be older than my years. Therefore I have been described as a precocious child. I drink coffee. I smoke cigarettes. I use the words: masturbatory, ennui, and existential — liberally in conversation. But today I am thirteen. I am wearing my sailor suit. I come down here often in my sailor suit, to the Howard Johnson's in Bloomfield, New Jersey and I wait. I wait for a man to come and take me away, away from this childhood that I do not belong in. A blonde man who is muscular and bold, I have seen him on TV. He will teach me how to be athletic and brave. He will give structure and meaning to my life. He will hold me in the dark. Just we two. I wait and wait. But he never seems to come. *(Boy lights a cigarette.)*

I was supposed to be bar mitzvahed today. But I told my mother I wouldn't go. I told her I had decided I didn't want to be Jewish anymore. My mother was distraught. "You can't just decide you don't want to be Jewish anymore," she said. I told her again, "I don't want to be Jewish." "Why don't you want to be Jewish?," she asked me. "In the street, children throw pennies at me, they call me Jew Bagel. In an age when it is possible for us to choose our destiny, I have decided I don't want to go through life with the particular disadvantage of

---

*See Special Note on Songs and Recordings on copyright page.

being a Jew. I want to be blonde and handsome like the men on TV. I want to drive a Volkswagen." "Over my dead body, you'll drive a Volkswagen. This wouldn't be happening if your father were alive." "He's not alive," I said, "he's dead!" My mother took a Valium and locked herself in her bedroom. *(Sound: a door slamming.)*

My father was a Jew. *(Boy lights another cigarette.)*

He came to America during World War Two. He was — an Alien. *(Music: Something like the music from "Psycho."*)*

He left behind his mother, sister, his first wife and a son. They died at Auswichz. I have here their names, as listed by the Red Cross. Rebecca, Betsy, Rachel, and the son, Wolf, who was shoveled into an oven on the day of his thirteenth birthday in 1943. *(Sound: Fire. Combustion. He burns the names of his relatives with flash paper.)*

I never got along with my father. He spoke with a heavy foreign accent. He was thin and pale and European, not at all like the men on TV. One day I was walking around the house in my mother's high heels and my father caught me. He slapped me and told me: "I never want you to walk in high heels again. Soon you will be thirteen, you will be bar mitzvahed, soon you will be a man." "I don't want to be a man," I told him. "*You're* a man, I wish you were dead." The next year he died of lung cancer. Now I wear my mother's high heels whenever she's not home. *(He puts on high heels. A song such as "I Feel Pretty,"* from* West Side Story *plays as the Alien Boy twirls.)*

I turn up the music from *West Side Story* and I twirl my baton. *(At some point in the music it stops with a screech and horror music fades in.)*

Last night after my mother had cooked me a Swanson's frozen TV dinner, I was reading *Everything You Always*

*See Special Note on Songs and Recordings on copyright page.

Wanted to Know about Sex but Were Afraid to Ask by David Reuben, M.D., and I quote:

VOICEOVER. "Male homosexuality is a condition in which men have a driving emotional and sexual interest in other men. Because of the anatomical and physiological limitations involved, there are some formidable obstacles to overcome. In the process they often transform themselves into part-time women. They don women's clothes, wear makeup, adopt feminine mannerisms, and occasionally even try to rearrange their bodies along feminine lines."

ALIEN BOY. I don't want to be a homosexual. Until last night I didn't know I was one. I knew I was different, but I didn't think there was a name for it. I knew I liked to wear my mother's slip. I knew I liked to wrestle with my friend Nicky Sabatino, and I knew I didn't mind losing. I knew I liked to rub against the sofa watching Monty Hall on *Let's Make A Deal*, and the cowboys on *Bonanza*. But then I read this:

VOICEOVER. "Some of the more routine items that find their way into the gastrointestinal systems of homosexuals via the exit are pens, pencils, lipsticks, combs, pop bottles, ladies electric shavers, and enough other items to stock a small department store." *(Sound: electric shaver.)*

ALIEN BOY. I definitely don't want to be a homosexual.

One day, after we finish wrestling, Nicky Sabatino tells me that there is a movie called *Boys in the Band*, about homos. I decide that I must see this movie, that perhaps it will shed light on this condition, this horrible thing that is me. I ask my mother to take me. I need her to take me because children are not permitted to see it unless accompanied by their legal guardian. "What's it about?" she asks. "About a group of musicians." "Why do you want to see it so bad?" "Because as you know, I am learning how to play the tuba, and my motivation is already failing because it's so hard to carry it back and forth to school." My mother agrees to take me because she would do anything to encourage my musicality. We go to the Royal Theater that night for the eight o'clock show. *(Music, such as Sousa music.*)*

When we get to the theater the woman who sells tickets will not let me in. She says the movie is unsuitable for children my age. I demand to see the manager. "It's illegal," I say, "what you're doing." The lady calls the manager. He is from a foreign country. He can't believe my mother would take me to see such a movie. "Do you know what it's about?," he asks her. "Musicians," she answers. He pulls her away from me and talks to her in hushed foreign tones. When she returns she tells me we can't enter, "I'm sorry, why don't we go to the Welmont Theater to see *Snow White and the Seven Dwarfs*? I start to throw a fit. "It's illegal, what they're doing," I say again, "I'm going to write a letter." My mother takes me across the street to Woolworths and offers to buy me a Hot Wheels set. "I don't want it," I say. I hold out until she buys me a GI Joe doll. She takes me home and makes me Jello.

The next evening I convince my mother that it is her civic responsibility to allow me to see *Boys in the Band*. "This is America," I remind her, "It's a free country." Finally, she agrees to take me to a theater in New York City, where we have no trouble attaining admittance. *(The lights dim, music: A song such as "Heatwave."*)*

As we sit in the darkness, I nervously eat a pack of Goobers and Raisinets. My mother fidgets and allows a pack of Eskimo Pies to melt uneaten onto her ecru pants suit. We watch together in horror as a group of genuine homosexuals complain about their mothers and dance together in a conga line — and as we watch, a subtle electricity flows back and forth

---

*See Special Note on Songs and Recordings on copyright page.

between my mother and myself, an unmistakable unspoken acknowledgment that now we both understand why I wanted to see this movie. When we leave the theater we are silent, in tacit agreement that we will not mention the horrible truth, that somewhere deep inside of us, we have both in this moment come to know. *(Sci-fi music plays. Lights flash outside the window.)*

That night I have a disturbing dream. Outside my window I see strange lights. A spaceship lands and a robot man descends from it's steps and comes into my bedroom. He is very blonde and looks like my GI Joe doll and the devastatingly handsome Nazis I have seen in war films. He comes to my bed and takes me on his lap. He looks very cold like metal but when he touches me his skin is hot. He holds me in his hot arms. He says that: "You must tell me that you love me." I look into his blonde eyes. I start to form the words I love you. "I ... love ..." I wake up screaming. *(Sound: A horror movie scream.)*

It's two in the morning. In *Boys in the Band,* all the homosexuals had psychiatrists. I creep into the kitchen and go for the *Yellow Pages.* I look under the letter P. I find the names of all psychiatrists in Bloomfield. There are only two. Dr. Kaplan and Dr. Casey. I choose Dr. Casey, because he sounds more attractive. I write him a brief letter:

"Dear Dr. Casey: I think I am a homosexual. I have no money. I cannot tell my mother. Please help me. I want to be cured."

I find a stamp in my mother's pocketbook. For the rest of the night I dream of my doctor. The one who will save me. The man I've been waiting for.

The next day while carrying my tuba, I mail the letter to my doctor. The boys at school stop calling me Jewboy and begin to call me pussy and faggot. I start to dress in work boots and flannel shirts to disguise myself. Anxious weeks pass as daily, I run home after school to check the mailbox. Every night I stay awake until four, praying to the God I do not believe in to save me from my sordid fate. Then one day a letter arrives, addressed to me. *(Music, such as Vicki Carr singing: "Dear God It Must Be Him."* The Alien Boy clutches the letter to his chest and opens it, his heart pounding.)*

He will see me one week from today in his office. I am filled with excruciating anticipation. The week passes quickly, and on the day of our assignation I run from school to the bus that will take me to my hero. I have dressed in my argyle shirt and socks, corduroy bell bottoms and platform shoes, tempting derogatory slurs from the boys in gym class, but I don't care, I am reckless with expectation.

I arrive at the address of Dr. Casey's office. I ring the bell and am buzzed into a small waiting room. "I'm here to see Dr. Casey," I say to the secretary with a hint of pride. As she knocks suspiciously on the doctor's door I look around his office. I am disappointed to find other people here. The secretary returns and ushers me into Dr. Casey's office. Suddenly as I am face to face with the man who knows my secrets, I realize why I have felt vaguely disoriented since arriving. Dr. Casey is a black person, like his secretary and the people in the waiting room. I am momentarily unable to process this information as I have never seen a black doctor on TV. But the look of kindness in his handsome face reassures me. I imagine my small white face pressed against his strong black chest. The secretary leaves and the doctor asks me a few questions. "Why do you think you're a homosexual?" "Because I like men," I tell him. "What do you want to do with them?" "I don't know," I say, "just be with them, and give them blow jobs," I offer, searching for the correct answers. "Where did you learn that word?" "In *Everything You Always Wanted To Know About Sex* by David

*See Special Note on Songs and Recordings on copyright page.

Reuben, M.D.," I reply. Dr. Casey seems satisfied with my answers and then rises from behind his desk. "I'd like to help you," he says, "But you understand I can't possibly treat you without the permission of your mother." *(Horror music.)*

He hands me the phone. "I'm afraid you'll have to call her and tell her where you are." *(Sound: Air raid sirens.)*

I dial my mother's phone number at work, unable to look him in the eyes. "Hello Mom?" "I'm at a doctor's office. No, nothing's wrong." *(Sound: Two trains crashing.)*

I hand the phone to Dr. Casey. "I think you should come down and pick your son up," he says. "313 Bloomfield Avenue." He hangs up the phone. I look into Dr. Casey's eyes. A moment of unbearable silence passes. *(Pause.)* "Nigger." *(The Boy puts his hands over his mouth. A beat.)*

My mother collects me at Dr. Casey's office and she tells him: "What he's lacking is a male role model." Dr. Casey agrees and offers to treat me, but my mother, nervously replies that "There is a Dr. Kaplan in Bloomfield, who I think would be a more appropriate choice for us." We walk briskly to the car. We sit in front of Dr. Casey's office in silence. *(Alien Boy, as Mother, lights a cigarette.)*

"Why didn't you tell me about this ... problem." "There is no problem, I feel better already." "Really, I think it's just a phase you're going through." "Yes, I feel it passing already as we speak." "What would you like for dinner?" "Can we go to McDonalds?" "Yes, I think that's a wonderful idea." *(Music, such as Muzak.*)*

As we sit in the shiny new McDonalds, my mother and I don't speak again about the phase I am going through. I sip my chocolate milkshake and my mother turns and asks me: "Do you want to talk to Dr. Kaplan?" "No, I hate psychiatrists."

---

*See Special Note on Songs and Recordings on copyright page.

She picks at her Filet-O-fish. "Maybe I should have remarried. Do you miss your father?" "No." She delicately chews on a French fry. "I miss him." She takes a gulp of Fresca. A moment passes. "I opened that letter you got from Dr. Casey, you know, saying he would see you. I made him have you call me from his office. I told him I'd sue him if he didn't. I'm sorry. Please forgive me. I didn't know what else to do. I love you." *(Sound: A beast roars.)*

"It's OK," I say. I stare at my hot apple pie. I start to form the words I love you. "I love ..." *(Music: A song such as "Heatwave"* bumps up.)* ... and suddenly I see the plastic chairs begin to melt. The table is bursting into fire. I smell the stench of burning flesh, and as McDonald's is consumed by flames I scream for help ... and all at once my dead father appears and takes my hand. He pulls my mother to her feet. With him is HIS mother and his first wife and their son Wolf. Dr. Casey joins us and David Reuben, M.D. ... and as the plastic burns around us, we begin to dance together. We form a huge conga line and we dance. We dance and we dance and we dance, through the flames.

LIGHTS FADE TO BLACK

---

*See Special Note on Songs and Recordings on copyright page.

PROPERTY LIST

Cigarette
Lighter or matches
Flash paper
Letter

SOUND EFFECTS

Nuclear bomb exploding
Door slamming
Fire and combustion
Electric shaver
Horror movie scream
Horror movie music
Air raid siren
2 trains crashing
Beast roaring

FIRE DANCE

FIRE DANCE

An African-American man enters in a conservative business suit. He addresses the audience. He speaks very quickly. Throughout he changes from his male drag into her full and divine female drag, makeup, pumps, wig and all. The transformation is efficient, rhythmic, and astonishing.

CRYSTAL.   Before I went on Prozac ... I used to be a very emotional person, hyper-sensitive you know, hysterical — and just forget about self-esteem. This used to make things hard for me, you know, like it would make it hard for me sometimes, to live in this world, to do the things that people need to do to — you know — live. For instance, like to go to the grocery store, or to mail a letter, you know, *NORMAL* things. I didn't even used to be able to go to the bank even, to stand on that line, to talk to the teller, it would get me — agitated. *(He begins to remove suit.)*

Now, I didn't think that this was always so bad of a thing though, at that particular time in my life — because what I was was — what I was — I was a creative person, you know, a performer. Uh-huhhh! I used to do shows at The Anvil and The Mineshaft — you remember those places, yes? Perhaps then you have even heard of me — Crystal was my name, Crystal Chandaliah — *(He waits for recognition.)*

Yes well — in my time, did I ever light up a stage — oh yes honey, I was electric. Fabulous. FLAMING! *(Lights pop on at makeup table.)*

You see, before I went on Prozac, I was the partner of The Amazing Nubia — now you *MUST* remember *HER* — She did the Fire Dance at The Anvil: the most famous act since

Carmen Miranda, the Salem Witch Trials, and Cher all rolled into one.

Oh yes — Nubia taught me everything I know about show business, she was like a sister to me, and her and me, we were like the hottest sister act in town. *(Puts on his makeup robe.)*

You *COULD* say that Nubia discovered me and you wouldn't be lying. She discovered me one night in 1975 at The Cockring, lying on the floor of the bathroom, with my wrists slit open and my dress slashed to pieces. What a mess, darling — bleeding all over that linoleum! Now what Nubia *DID* — what she did was ... this is what she did: she ripped off her gold lame sash, tied it around my arms and stopped off the bleeding! Next day I woke up in her cold-water apartment on Christopher Street, Donna Summers was singing on the radio, and Nubia fed me on rose hips tea. She called herself Miss Nurse ... and for two weeks she didn't get out of her stunning white nursing ensemble with matching white pumps. *She saved my life!* And she taught me how to Fire Dance. She said: "Honey, if you gotta burn — make 'em pay to see it." *(Begins to put on makeup.)*

Nubia was the mother of all drag queens. They don't make 'em like that anymore. She was the first queen to throw a bottle at the cops during the Stonewall Rebellion. Other queens invented the word, FIERCE, just to describe her. It has even been rumored that Nubia was the first homosexual ever to snap her fingers *(She snaps.)* and the phrase: "I will read your beads, Miss Mary Dugan!" has been attributed to her. *(He does his eyes, rouge and cheekbones.)*

Nubia taught me that to do the Fire Dance you gotta have a ... VENEER, you know what I'm talking about? One day she says to me: "Honey — honey — you best be gettin' yourself some VENEER! else you gonna wind up on that bathroom floor again!" "VENEER?" I says to her. "VENEER," she says, "like you know, like a ... like a SHEEN, you see, 'cause let me tell you something, Miss Thing Girl: It ain't easy doin' the Fire Dance, bein' a drag queen, livin' the life. Uh-uh — No, darlin'." And Nubia was right. *(Lipwork.)*

It seems these days everybody and her mother wants to be a drag queen, how funny you know, when all I ever wanted was just to be a *NORMAL* person, like y'all. I mean sure it may LOOK glamorous, but it's an awful lot of work to make yourself over! I mean let all the other queens sing "I AM WHAT I AM," but drag queens we sing "I AM WHAT I AM NOT," you know what I'm sayin'? *(Powder and final touches.)*

Uh-uh. Tsk tsk tsk: I even hear that Mr. Patrick Swayze is dressin' himself up for some big Hollywood type movie about drag queens — well I got some advice for you Mr. Patrick Swayze honey: You best be doin' some serious research about givin' good head, pardon my French, because if you are a drag queen and you can't be giving some serious head, you might as well just take off that lipstick right now, girlfriend! *(Final lip outline; gets into stockings, breasts, dress.)*

Oh yes. Nubia taught me how to have a fierce veneer. Sometimes we danced the Fire Dance five or six times a night. Twirling our fiery batons to Pearl Bailey's rendition of "Hot Voodoo," lip synching to Martha and the Vandella's cover of "Heatwave," glittering in our sequined dresses, our amazing black bodies shimmering under the virgin olive oil that we had so carefully applied before the show to protect us from the heat. But to tell you the truth, underneath my veneer — I still dreamed of a normal life — like married to some nice blonde republican, like George Bush's nephew ... a life in which I went to the bank without fear, in which I balanced my checkbook, a life in which I cooked my man dinner and cleaned his kitchen, but Nubia said: "You're crazy girl! Don't even think such thoughts. That life ain't never gonna be for you. But you know, The real fact is, I loved Nubia. Not in a sexy way. But I really loved her. More than the guys from Greenpoint who I did in the back seats of their white Continentals. The guys who I couldn't stop loving even though they used to beat me up after, more than them, more than myself even, I loved her.

And I loved the Fire Dance, the life of dancin' the Fire Dance with abandon, unafraid. *(Lights shift.)*

Then one night in the middle of a performance I looked on as suddenly, Nubia's amazing black body was consumed by flames. A freak accident. Her skin blazing like some highly flammable material, which no one could put out, no matter how we tried. Sometimes I see her face looking up at me, as it did at that moment, and I swear it was like she was almost smiling through the pain. The crowd was going crazy around us, screaming and wailing, but I felt almost calm as I looked into Nubia's smiling face, as if she was saying to me what she had said a hundred thousand times to me before: "Crystal, if you do the Fire Dance, you gotta be prepared to burn." *(Finishing touches on costume, boa, jewels.)*

Next day I went to a Chemical Bank and I opened a checking account. I went to a Dr. Casey, a very nice man, who put me on Prozac. That was five years ago and I've never looked back. Today, I am a *normal* person. A happy person. I really really am! I work as a word processor in a small law firm. I live with my boyfriend in New Jersey. He's a chemical engineer at Hoffman-La Roche Labs and he gets me my Prozac for free.

Nowadays my life is good! On Saturdays I shop at Shop-Rite. On Sundays I iron my shirt to get ready for work. And I balance my checkbook once a week! *(Wig, and then finished, a vision, she presents herself to the crowd.)*

I don't dance the Fire Dance anymore. Sometimes when I go to the city, I'll run into one of the girls on the street, and they'll ask me if I don't miss performing. I tell then no, and it's true: I don't miss the Fire Dance. But sometimes late at night, around two in the morning, when my night shift's done and I can't sleep, I sneak into the bathroom. I close the door and I light many candles — *(Lights candles, spotlight focuses on her.)*

    — and I stare at my face in the mirror ... And as I stare into the flames of the candles flickering around me I begin to sing, I sing in my own voice. I sing for Nubia, for all the girls, for myself I sing, this is what I tell us *(Smoke billows around her as she sings a song like Aretha Franklin's, "I Say a Little Prayer ..."* Lights fade.)*

*See Special Note on Songs and Recordings on copyright page.

PROPERTY LIST

Makeup
Robe
Wig
Stockings
Breasts
Dress
Boa
Jewels
Candles
Lighter or matches

TENNESSEE AND ME

TENNESSEE AND ME

Music such as the theme from Gone with the Wind* *plays as a large bathtub rolls onto stage. Me inside the tub surrounded by candles. He is mixing martinis. He speaks with a heavy New York accent.*

ME. On February 25th, 1983, at approximately 2:00 in the morning, while taking a hot bath in his suite at the Hotel Elysee, the great playwright and notoriously alcoholic homosexual, Tennessee Williams, died amidst the bubbles, asphyxiated by the cap of a pill vial, lodged in his throat.

It so happens that on that same unfortunate morning about an hour earlier, I — who at that time was a rather inarticulate male prostitute from Bensonhurst, Brooklyn — was running naked through the lobby of the Holiday Inn on 48th street, having just extinguished a cigarette in the sagging white belly of a Pulitzer Prize-winning poet, who had paid me five hundred dollars to do so, but who now seemed to be suffering from mild cardiac arrest apparently brought on by my action.

Grasping my five hundred dollars but foregoing my clothes I ran from the hotel and lunged into a waiting taxi and throwing a one hundred dollar bill into the front seat ordered the gaping cabby to take me to the St. Marks Baths, a popular gay bathhouse on the lower east side that flourished in the innocent age before the plague had come to live with us in this city of strangers.

Upon checking into the baths that night I procured for myself the honeymoon suite. The only room in the entire place with a double bed, and quickly finding a dealer that I fre-

*See Special Note on Songs and Recordings on copyright page.

quented at this establishment, bought for myself a variety of pills that would serve various purposes for the time I expected to stay there. In the spa room which contained a large and fairly clean Jacuzzi, after having popped a few brightly colored pills I attracted the attention of an attractive blonde bodied fellow with a mustache and highly developed pectoral muscles, which had recently come into fashion. He wore only a towel and workboots. Affecting my most masculine demeanor, which I had perfected through years of rigorous conditioning, I was able to lure this paragon of manhood back to my room. After sharing a joint, and carefully avoiding any conversation that might break the spell, we went at satisfying our obviously mutual desire. After approximately fifteen minutes, and at precisely 2:00 A.M., exactly as uptown from us Mr. Williams was choking in his tub, I began to come.

And for a reason that till this day must remain a mystery to me — all at once I was coming and screaming and choking and yelling: "Oh baby, oh baby," in a ridiculously southern accent that stuck foreignly in my throat. As I watched my new buddy stare at me with obvious discomfort, I tried to apologize for my sudden and embarrassing display, but all that came out of my mouth was a high pitched cackle, and without being able to stop myself, I heard myself say: "Oh baby that was just *fabulous* — now why don't you run on down to the corner drugstore and get me a nice lemon Coke with lots of shaved ice."

My blonde friend fled screaming from the honeymoon suite and I, badly shaken, staggered to the mirror and stared in shock and horror at what I saw reflected there, for the eyes that stared back at me were not my own, and I knew somehow quite clearly, that in one shining instant, oblivious as to how and why he had chosen me, the soul of Tennessee Williams had leapt into my body like a candle flame leaping into the dark night; I was possessed. *(Tubular bells play.)*

ME. "What are you doing?"
TENNESSEE. "I'm moving in baby."
ME. "You can't move in. Get out of me!"
TENNESSEE. "But honey — we've had this date with each other from the beginning."
ME. "Why do you have to move into me?"
TENNESSEE. "I've come back for love, baby ... and you have the body to get it for me."
ME. "I don't even know who you are!"
TENNESSEE. "Jus' hush up then sweetie ... I've always depended on the kindness of strangers."

This was indeed a predicament of major proportions for me, as I had practiced a lifetime avoiding such flagrant effeminacy. And so fleeing from the baths after obtaining some clothes I instinctively searched for the nearest Catholic church, believing exorcism to be my only hope.

When I entered the Church of the Heavenly Mother on third street it was empty, save for a rather young and attractive priest who was wearing a simple black habit and swinging a smoking incense burner over the altar. I ran to him, genuflecting at his feet. I was about to explain my unfortunate situation when Tennessee who was putting up a tremendous fight to inhabit me, lurched into high gear. And again unable to control myself, while looking the priest up and down, I intoned: "DAHLING, I love your dress but your bag's on fire." Expecting the priest to take grave offense I cringed before him. But I was surprised when I heard him let out a fluttering shriek of a laugh, and next thing I knew he had whisked me into a confessional and began to perform an unspeakable act on me with great gusto and positively religious fervor. It wasn't long before I felt myself tremble with ecstasy and again Tennessee's voice sighed unbidden from my lips: "Oh baby — sometimes there's God — so quickly." And soon it was quite clear to me that this Tennessee Williams was planning to move in for good. I began to speak with a southern accent even as I despised his presence inside me. *(Southern accent creeps in.)*

He dragged me to bar after bar in search of love, to all the bars I had frequented before to earn my living. Sometimes he would have me affect my most unavailable demeanor, and on those nights we were remarkably successful at winning the sexual favors of boys of all different colors shapes and sizes. However there were nights when Tennessee would get bored and invite Truman Capote, who was recently deceased, to join us in my body — at which times I would sit at the bar carrying on lisping conversations with myself:

TRUMAN. "But you know, Tom, that the only thing that men hate more than women is homosexuals!"
TENNESSEE. "Yes baby, and the only thing that homosexuals hate more than women is themselves! *(Truman — a lisping laugh.)* Please Mary. You're completely destroyin' our image as the strong silent type."

But it really didn't matter. Any way we played it, the elusive love that Tennessee had come back for, continued to elude us. I however became used to having Tennessee in my body. We had a strange sort of marriage, and for the first time in my life I experienced a more delicate sensibility. I became morose, I began to think about the sadness of the world. I bought a typewriter and started to write bad plays which Tennessee criticized unmercifully.

Then one night the impossible happened. We both fell in love with the same boy. A bright particular boy. Tennessee made me kiss him ... right on the mouth. Something I had never done before, not even for money — because I guess I knew that it would make me a *real* homosexual. And the boy kissed back with sincerity. And I found that I liked it.

The object of our mutual infatuation was Freddy, who

was in all ways a delight to behold, both in appearance and personality. I suppose Freddy was a notoriously modern homosexual. You know the kind: full of himself, unashamed, in your face ... beautiful. He seemed actually to contain a wholeness of qualities that might best be described as a self. And the tragedy was: that Freddy really did love us. And I came to understand that this love was unacceptable to Tennessee and me. It was not long after that, while taking a bath, that Tennessee told me he was departing.

TENNESSEE. "It's all loss here honey, and I could never bear it. Never then and never now, but thank you for the ride."

ME. "Please don't leave me Tenn. I'm just street trash without you."

TENNESSEE. "No you're not baby, you just need to take hold of yourself — and gently, gently with love, hand your life back to yourself."

And then he was gone — flying up, up in his bathtub, and into the night. Now I live alone. But there is something of Tennessee that remains with me still. A longing, a nostalgia for a time that will never be again. I might even go so far as to say that I miss those old days. Perhaps I am walking on the streets of this city, and I pass the old location of a bar or a nightclub that we used to frequent. Or perhaps I hear a familiar strain of music, a Donna Summers song, and the memories of that time rush back upon me, like the crystalline lights of a mirrored disco ball, like a thousand pieces of broken glass — Oh Tennessee I tried to forget you. But it's been harder than I ever thought it would be. For nowadays the world is lit by lightning, so blow out your candles Tennessee. And so good-bye. *(Me blows out the candles around the bathtub. Blackout. Music such as Donna Summer's: "Last Dance"* plays.)*

---

*See Special Note on Songs and Recordings on copyright page.

PROPERTY LIST

Martini paraphernalia
Candles

SOUND EFFECTS

Tubular bells

ONE MAN'S MEAT

ONE MAN'S MEAT

Music such as "Dancing Cheek to Cheek"* plays as the lights come up on a handsome young man wearing a tuxedo. He is in a beautiful kitchen somewhere in heaven. He is always charming and poised, with a delightful sense of humor.

J.D. Welcome to: Cooking with Jeffrey Dahmer. *(He swirls and sips a glass of sherry. Dances a pirouette.)*

Isn't this kitchen beautiful? A little bit of heaven. A place inextricably linked to … love. Mother's love. Unconditional love. The love of potentiality. Of possibility. Of preparation. A place of love that is entirely metaphysical. A somewhere where, we are reminded of how much, in our lives, we have loved purely. A place where I am reminded now, that I need make no apologies for my life, because, indeed, I have loved so much more than most. In truth, I have. *(He dons an immaculate white apron.)*

And so today: HOW TO KEEP A MAN. *(He smiles and places a very large, heavy pot onto the stove.)*

An eminently worthwhile question, don't you think? How many times did I remind myself, in my own little kitchen on earth, amidst the pots, the pans, the implements, the spices: that, the way to a man's heart was through his stomach. *(He picks up a large knife.)*

Literally. *(He begins to chop onions, expertly and quickly.)*

And how many times did I feel there, so keenly, in my little kitchen, that the knife of love must cut both ways. *(Wipes a tear from his eye.)*

---

*See Special Note on Songs and Recordings on copyright page.

But let's get down to business. You see, when I was a little boy, my mother took me to Cincinnati, to view a lovely production of *South Pacific*. After the show, she asked me what, if anything, the show had taught me about life. Without a pause, and in my fine young tenor voice, I responded: *(He sings.)* "Once you have found him never let him go. Once you have found him ne-ver let him gooooo." My mother smiled her approval, because, well ... but of course, isn't that the goal of life? To love someone forever, eternally, completely. To never ever let them go. I think so. And therefore the question does arise, for oh so many of us: HOW DOES ONE KEEP A MAN? *(He throws the onions into the pot. He sips his sherry.)*

I just simply adore recipes, don't you? The intricacy of their ingredients. The intimacy of remembering their every detail. The inevitability of their timing. Each one like a little destiny in itself, that if followed to the letter, with a perfect pinch of this, a delicate dash of that, must lead us to our destination. Our end. The word made ... flesh. Oh yes, I love everything about recipes. *(He throws a large slab of meat onto the cutting board.)* A recipe, you see, is an act of ... remembrance. *(He begins to remove the fat.)*

And to re-member is to give meaning to. Quite literally, to put together again. And to put together again, one must first dis-member. To take apart. And so it is, that in a sense, we must both dis-member and re-member, to give meaning. We must both take apart and then put together again, to make sense of our fragile selves. *(He produces a butcher's knife.)*

It's funny, in life, some people prefer to forget and some to remember. Myself, I prefer to remember. To remember every little detail. The way for instance, the hand of the one you love rests upon a table, in repose. *(He begins to hack the meat apart.)*

The sweet smell of their neck. Like milk. The unforgettable taste of their lips. To remember each part of them, so that in remembering, your love will never die. *(He places the pieces of meat into the pot.)*

But oh my, I have digressed too far. Some might even say, transgressed. *(Beat.)* So to continue: HOW TO KEEP A MAN. Pencils ready?? *(He puts on rubber gloves.)*

Of course to keep a man, one must first catch a man. Dad always used to say that, before they met, Mom used to eat her men for breakfast. He was speaking figuratively of course, but it made an impression on me. And it is true. My mother had many admirers as a young girl. But when she met my father, I think she believed she had found the ONE. The one that would be hers forever. For better or for worse, for richer or poorer, in sickness and in health, till death do us part. *(He pours a liquid carefully into his pot. It bubbles like a cauldron.)*

But you see, the world has no use for such ritual anymore. No respect for symbolic contracts. No understanding of the subtle interplay between the spiritual and the material, the intermingling of spirit and flesh. When my parents were divorced in 1978, torn asunder, as it were, this too made a strong impression. I am not moralizing mind you, far be it from me to do that, but just observing from my airy heights. For it has become so clear to me, from this perspective, that the only way to keep a man, to love a man, in a world of opposites, is just ... to love him. To love him to the depth and breadth and height your soul can reach. And if need be, now I understand, to love him and to let him go. And to love that deeply, that completely, so to speak, is a mystery, the recipe for which may have never been. Or at least one which has vanished from our tawdry times, in which we seem to see only the black or the white, the good or the evil, the sugar or the salt. Whereas the proportions of real love must always be of equal parts both spirit and matter, a balance between the darkness and the light. *(He adds some spices to his brew.)*

And so perhaps, it was inevitable that I would have erred in the proportions of my recipe for love on earth, for of course in reality, there is none. And one must find the balance of love's violence and love's beauty for one's self. To create its recipe from scratch, as it were, and often times with very little guidance. *(He sips a spoonful of the broth.)*

And so, in closing, I ask you not to understand, not to make sense of, nor even to forgive me of my trespasses. But as we share this meal together, which I have prepared for you, I ask you to throw away your pencils and your preconceptions. And I ask you to accept me as an ingredient in the recipe of who you are yourselves. A dark but very human impulse deep inside you. A mystery buried somewhere in your hearts. For I am just someone who has loved, as you have loved, imperfectly. Someone who will always be with you, as if we were one soul. And so I say this unto you, in recognition of our "oneness": *(He plunges his hands into his pot and holds up a skull. Lights shift. Music swells.)*

"Take, eat, this is my body. Which I now give to you for the forgiveness of our sins. Do this in remembrance of me." *(He offers the meal to all. There is a long pause. Silence.)* No? *(Beat.)* I see. *(He places the skull away and wipes his hands clean on his apron.)*

You know, from this great height, in my clean and glittering kitchen, high above the cities of America, in this chill pure air of beauty, I look down upon you all, and I see you cooking in your little kitchens. And as I watch, I send down my blessings upon you. And I offer you this final word of advice. I ask you to follow *your* recipe well. I remind you to love both carefully and wisely, using the proper proportions of both heaven and earth. For surely I will come again, if you do not prepare the way. *(Thunder. And then music such as Sting's, "If You Love Somebody Set Them Free"* plays as the lights fade.)*

*See Special Note on Songs and Recordings on copyright page.

PROPERTY LIST

Glass of sherry
White apron
Heavy pot
Large knife
Onions
Cutting board
Large piece of meat
Butcher's knife
Rubber gloves
Liquid
Spices
Spoon
Skull

SOUND EFFECTS

Thunder

FALLING MAN

FALLING MAN

Wind.

The sound of air, as it rushes past ears. Lights come up on a Falling Man. His hair flies up in the wind. He is thin and his skin is very white. He wears underwear. He is falling. White clouds float behind him.

FALLING MAN.   You get used to the sound of the wind as it rushes past your ears. And the ominous sense of velocity becomes familiar after a while. You watch as the stars whiz by you like flying candles. You listen to the planets as they sing their songs. You think to yourself, at any moment I am going to come crashing down into the Earth, but you never do. At least not yet. *(Wind.)*

You begin to wonder about gravity. You become obsessed with it. You say to yourself over and over: I'm falling I'm falling, but soon you get used to not having your feet on the ground anymore. In fact, ground itself, becomes a concept that no longer has any meaning to you. *(Wind.)*

For some reason you can't seem to stop talking, as if talking were the only action that could give you your bearings in a constantly shifting environment without recognizable landmarks. You convince yourself that if you are talking, if someone can hear you, you must still be alive. You scream: I'm alive I'm alive, to no one in particular. You discover that you don't like to look down, but prefer to look up, for obvious reasons. And then quite suddenly, for a moment, without warning: you have this unbearable urge to cha cha once more. *(Blackout. cha cha music. When the lights come up again Falling Man sits on a chair in a pool of light. He wears a hospital gown and addresses the audience. Occasionally he operates a slide projector.)*

Before I started falling, I was a ballroom dancing champion, expert at ten dances. They were, in order of my expertise and preference: cha cha, salsa, mambo, samba, paso doblé, rhumba, tango, slow waltz, quick waltz and fox trot. On a perfect night in 1983, at the age of 22, I became the cha cha champion of the world. *(Slide: Falling Man at 22. TA DA!)* No one much remembers that now, but it's true. Even before this, however, I was famous for my cha cha. My dancing partner Svetlana defected from the former Soviet Union in 1981, specifically to dance the cha cha with me. And, at that time, we were legendary. You would have loved Svetlana. *(Slide: Svetlana, a big Soviet girl!)* She had an accent just like Norma Shearer in *Idiot's Delight*. You know, all vonderfuls and werys. "I am so wery wery crazy about you," she would often say to me. Sometimes I wondered if she had actually defected from Russia or if she hadn't really just hitchhiked to Manhattan from Deluth and made the whole thing up. But she was acknowledged to be the Soviet champion of the jive-rock step, *(Slide: Svetlana dancing!)* a dance step that for some reason only Baltic women could master. That and the fact that only Svetlana could really look sexy in Jordache jeans, wearing a shade of lipstick that was five times too red for even the most fabulous 1940's movie star, proved to me, at least, that she was genuinely Eastern European. *(Man in Black enters, wheeling an intravenous stand and proceeds to attach the hook-up to Falling Man's arm. Falling Man pauses for moment and then continues. Note: Man in Black is optional.))*

As I said before, we won the title of cha cha champions of the world on a perfect night in January of 1983. *(Slide: Falling Man and Svetlana. The winners!)* And we, indeed, ourselves, were perfect that night, as we moved across the dance floor of the Cincinnati Hilton Hotel. The floor was so highly polished that a few couples actually fell that evening. But not us. My strong arms that night, supported Svetlana in poses of inspired and delirious sexuality. *(Slide: Dancing!)* Our footwork was impeccable and unrivaled. We glittered and sparkled and shined. And of course, although the steps we navigated on that mirror smooth floor were uncompromisingly difficult — we did not once stumble or trip, or even slip or falter. *(Inspired, Falling Man rises to his feet.)*

Perhaps there could have been more of a natural passion between us, yes, but our acting was flawless and inspired. Not for a second was there a false move to our grace, to our speed and authority. And I now realize that in my life up until that moment there had never ever been even the remotest possibility of falling. It wasn't even a question. I would not have allowed it. I was not that kind of a person. No. *(Music fades up as Falling Man dances with the intravenous stand.)*

That night we floated, Svetlana and I. We glided. We dazzled. And for a moment, at the very climax of our passionate cha cha embrace, when I heard the entire crowd gasp together at our impossible beauty — I was almost happy. *(Applause. Man in Black enters and escorts him back to the chair. Man in Black removes the intravenous hook-up.)*

You must forgive me for talking so much. It's just that since I — started falling — I don't dance anymore. And so it seems I'm endlessly talking, endlessly meandering on about my past as a dancer. I hope I'm not boring you. Really all I'd like to do is to entertain you. You see, that's what ballroom dancing is really about, it's — entertainment and — it makes people feel good about life, about living, about being alive, do you know? And I am a born entertainer. I even used to dance to *West Side Story*, as a child, for the relatives. My mother encouraged me. As a matter of fact, I'd like to entertain you right now, even in my condition, as it were. Yes! That's what I'd really like to do, more than anything else. "Oh, I'd like to do a cha cha but the lesions hurt my feet!" *(He laughs.)* Sorry. Bad joke. Anyway. That night, Svetlana and I celebrated in my hotel room. *(Man in Black gives Falling Man a sip of water from a glass with a straw.)*

We drank champagne from Svetlana's silver cha cha slipper, which she stained red with her lips. We got drunk, and before Svetlana could stain me red, I convinced her that we should make an appearance at the post competition party in the Buck Eye Room of the Cincinnati Hilton. *(Man in Black escorts Falling Man to another chair, lights shift. There is a basin beneath the chair. Throughout the following Man in Black will gently and delicately sponge bathe Falling Man. The action should be slow and intimate.)*

When we made our entrance the party was in full swing and the waves seemed to part for us, as we made our way into the room. Compliments flowed endlessly along with the alcohol but I felt vaguely uncomfortable that night with Svetlana on my arm. Sometimes it seems to me that Destiny has a way of making you ready for her arrival. Of creating the conditions necessary for her to be able to play out her cards. Because I can't explain why I felt, as I did at that moment, at that exact moment in the Buck Eye Room of the Cincinnati Hilton Hotel on the night of my triumphant cha cha, that my young life until then had been nothing more than a championship performance, a perfect ten absolutely, but just a performance nonetheless. A graceful, well choreographed, impeccable dance for the relatives. And no sooner than I had this impression, or rather as I was having it, I saw an enchanting stranger from across the room, the crowded room as it were, and our eyes locked. He was not precisely a stranger, for I recognized him, although I had never met him, as Paolo, a Brazilian dancer, whose mambo I had appreciated. You might find this hard to believe, but I must admit to you now, that at the ripe age of 22 and even in that day and time, I was still a virgin on that fateful night in Cincinnati, in 1983. And as Paolo and I slowly and inexorably made our way towards each other, my heart beat with a fear experienced perhaps only by 22-year-old virgins, who have never entirely admitted to themselves that they are homosexual — and their mothers. But there was no turning back. Destiny had opened her arms wide to greet me and soon so had Paolo, who kissed me warmly on both cheeks with congratulations. This action on his part caused an immediate and uncontrollable erection on my part, so to speak. And I understood by the look in Paolo's eyes that indeed he, had coveted my cha cha as much as I had admired his mambo. Quickly and without too much effort I lost Svetlana, who was demonstrating the jive-rock step to a group of enthusiastic older men, and made my way to Paolo's room. *(As the lights shift, Man in Black lights a candle and puts a record on a small record player. A very romantic Brazilian samba* begins to play softly. Falling Man continues to speak to the audience.)*

I don't really know how to put into words what happened next. If I could I would dance it for you; I would dance that night for you and not trivialize it with words. After all, Paolo and I barely spoke ourselves. Sometimes I think love is about inventing a private language, a language lovers makeup as they go along, that only they can speak and understand — isn't that what love is? Just a language, an intricate intoxicating language that you have forgotten and now you must remember. But surely you understand what I am saying? That night almost immediately upon entering his room, I fell into Paolo's arms and we began to dance. *(Falling Man dances with Man in Black.)*

---

*See Special Note on Songs and Recordings on copyright page.

That was the language we spoke all that night. A language that was all our own. We danced our words as if our tongues had been burned from our mouths. *(Falling Man removes Man in Black's shirt.)*

I wonder if you can understand what that felt like to me — please try to understand because tonight I want us to be like lovers — but I wonder if you can, can know what it felt like for me to dance the cha cha with him. I who was the champion of the world in that dance. To dance the samba, the mambo, the tango with him. To dance with a man. For me, who had danced a thousand sambas, with a thousand lovely women, in a thousand sparkling rooms, for me, to dance with a man for the first time in my life. *(Falling Man lets his robe fall to the ground.)*

How can I explain to you. How can I describe it as I fell. As I fell for the first time in my young life. As I fell into the eyes of him, as I fell into the deep of his smell, into the strong arms of him, into his mouth. As we fell into each other. *(They kiss.)*

As we danced. *(After a moment, Falling Man removes the record with a scratch and they freeze. Falling Man puts on his robe and comes down to talk to the audience. Man in Black stands behind him.)*

You must forgive me. You must forgive me for talking so much. I know it's silly but sometimes I think if I stop talking I'll die. That you will forget me. That you will forget that I was a champion dancer, expert at ten dances, cha cha, salsa, mambo, samba, paso doblé, rhumba, tango, slow waltz, quick waltz and fox trot, in order of my preference. I am afraid you will forget me and my cha cha. I am afraid that you will judge me. That you will condemn me for falling that night. That astonishing night in 1983. I want so much to entertain you, but you must understand, that night, it was as if I had to fall. As if a person like me had just been waiting to fall all his life. And it felt not so much as if I were falling, but more like I was being born, but of course you understand that, don't you? *(Long pause.)*

I'm afraid I must be boring you. I'm afraid I'm running out of time. I'll just tell you this. Paolo died a year later. *(Man in Black exits.)*

It was so fast. I didn't even have a chance to learn Portuguese. Not long after that, Svetlana took me to the clinic to get tested. And I've been falling ever since. *(Black out. Wind. Gentle cha cha music such as that from* West Side Story.* *Lights come up again on Falling Man. Stars twinkle behind him.)*

You know, sometimes I see the other falling people around me and I want to grab onto them as we fall. I want to dance with them up here in the sky. I want to choreograph some fabulous Busby Berkeley type number up here in the sky. So everyone can look up and just see these fabulous falling people. I think that would be terrific, but it's so hard to organize. *(Wind.)*

I have to stop talking. I do have one thing to ask you, though. When I am finished talking, remember that I used to dance the cha cha, that I was the cha cha champion of the world. And remember the sound of my voice — so that all of this talking will not have been in vain. Remember my cha cha. Remember my voice. Remember me. *(The sound of the wind rises. Lights fade. Blackout.)*

END OF PLAY

---

*See Special Note on Songs and Recordings on copyright page.

PROPERTY LIST

Slide projector
Glass of water with straw
Basin
Sponge
Record
Candle
Lighter or matches

SOUND EFFECTS

Wind
Cha cha music

NEW PLAYS

- **TAKING SIDES by Ronald Harwood.** Based on the true story of one of the world's greatest conductors whose wartime decision to remain in Germany brought him under the scrutiny of a U.S. Army determined to prove him a Nazi. *"A brave, wise and deeply moving play delineating the confrontation between culture, and power, between art and politics, between irresponsible freedom and responsible compromise."* --London Sunday Times. [4M, 3W] ISBN: 0-8222-1566-7

- **MISSING/KISSING by John Patrick Shanley.** Two biting short comedies, MISSING MARISA and KISSING CHRISTINE, by one of America's foremost dramatists and the Academy Award winning author of *Moonstruck*. *" ... Shanley has an unusual talent for situations ... and a sure gift for a kind of inner dialogue in which people talk their hearts as well as their minds...."* --N.Y. Post. MISSING MARISA [2M], KISSING CHRISTINE [1M, 2W] ISBN: 0-8222-1590-X

- **THE SISTERS ROSENSWEIG by Wendy Wasserstein**, Pulitzer Prize-winning author of *The Heidi Chronicles*. Winner of the 1993 Outer Critics Circle Award for Best Broadway Play. A captivating portrait of three disparate sisters reuniting after a lengthy separation on the eldest's 50th birthday. *"The laughter is all but continuous."* --New Yorker. *"Funny. Observant. A play with wit as well as acumen.... In dealing with social and cultural paradoxes, Ms. Wasserstein is, as always, the most astute of commentators."* --N.Y. Times. [4M, 4W] ISBN: 0-8222-1348-6

- **MASTER CLASS by Terrence McNally. Winner of the 1996 Tony Award for Best Play.** Only a year after winning the Tony Award for *Love! Valour! Compassion!*, Terrence McNally scores again with the most celebrated play of the year, an unforgettable portrait of Maria Callas, our century's greatest opera diva. *"One of the white-hot moments of contemporary theatre. A total triumph."* --N.Y. Post. *"Blazingly theatrical."* -- USA Today. [3M, 3W] ISBN: 0-8222-1521-7

- **DEALER'S CHOICE by Patrick Marber.** A weekly poker game pits a son addicted to gambling against his own father, who also has a problem but won't admit it. *"... make tracks to DEALER'S CHOICE, Patrick Marber's wonderfully masculine, razor-sharp dissection of poker-as-life.... It's a play that comes out swinging and never lets up -- a witty, wisecracking drama that relentlessly probes the tortured souls of its six very distinctive ... characters. CHOICE is a cutthroat pleasure that you won't want to miss."* --Time Out (New York). [6M] ISBN: 0-8222-1616-7

- **RIFF RAFF by Laurence Fishburne.** RIFF RAFF marks the playwriting debut of one of Hollywood's most exciting and versatile actors. *"Mr. Fishburne is surprisingly and effectively understated, with scalding bubbles of anxiety breaking through the surface of a numbed calm."* --N.Y. Times. *"Fishburne has a talent and a quality...[he] possesses one of the vital requirements of a playwright -- a good ear for the things people say and the way they say them."* --N.Y. Post. [3M] ISBN: 0-8222-1545-4

DRAMATISTS PLAY SERVICE, INC.
440 Park Avenue South, New York, NY 10016 212-683-8960 Fax 212-213-1539
postmaster@dramatists.com www.dramatists.com